Ivan Gibbons

DRAWING THE LINE

The Irish Border in British Politics

First published by Haus Publishing in 2018
4 Cinnamon Row
London SW11 3TW
www.hauspublishing.com

A CIP catalogue record for this book is
available from the British Library

Print ISBN: 978-1-912208-29-6
Ebook ISBN: 978-1-912208-30-2

Typeset in Garamond by MacGuru Ltd

Printed in Spain

Contents

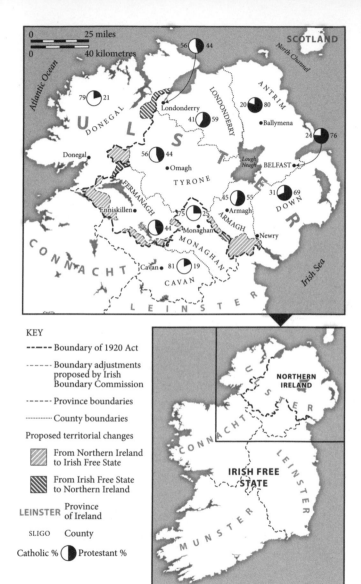

KEY

- - - - Boundary of 1920 Act

- - - - - - Boundary adjustments proposed by Irish Boundary Commission

- - - - - Province boundaries

.... County boundaries

Proposed territorial changes

From Northern Ireland to Irish Free State

From Irish Free State to Northern Ireland

LEINSTER Province of Ireland

SLIGO County

Catholic % Protestant %

Population data from Eilis Brennan and Sandra Gillespie, *Nationalism and Unionism* (Cambridge University Press, 1996), p. 74

Chronology

Introduction

When Thomas Agar-Robartes, Liberal MP for St Austell, moved an amendment to the Third Home Rule Bill in June 1912 proposing that the counties Londonderry, Down, Antrim and Armagh should be excluded from the proposed Irish Home Rule settlement, he unwittingly set in motion a process that was to have a profound political impact on the island of Ireland as well as its relationship with Britain for the remainder of the twentieth century and beyond – and still does. Why, after nearly a hundred years in existence, is the Irish border once again at the heart of our politics? It's a question which has led to much bewilderment and is the obvious reason for this book, as the answer can only be explained through an understanding as to why and how the Irish border was established in the first place.

Agar-Robartes was the first British politician to formally propose the partition of Ireland and the establishment of an Irish border. His proposal was an attempt to respond to the growing opposition to Home Rule from, in particular, Ulster unionists. He was killed at the Battle of Loos in Northern France three years later, in the early stages of the First World War, and so never lived to see the consequences of his amendment. In 1912, however, his amendment was greeted with

outrage by all political parties. Both British and Irish politicians, irrespective of party, regarded his proposal as an assault
on the constitutional integrity of both the UK and Ireland.
Agar-Robartes was merely expressing a growing frustration
at the seemingly intractable impasse between Irish nationalists and Irish (specifically Ulster) unionists as to what should
be the future constitutional status of Ireland. In this he was
merely ahead of his time.

In 1912, all three British political parties that were to
dominate British politics over the course of the twentieth
century continued to attach significant importance to maintaining their links with Irish politics of one sort or another:
the Liberals because of the lingering shadow of Gladstonian
commitment to Irish Home Rule dating back more than a generation (and, more prosaically, because of their dependence
on Irish Home Rule MPs to maintain a Liberal majority at
Westminster after the 1910 general elections); the Tories
because they shared ideological beliefs with Irish unionism
on the importance of monarchy, religion and the preservation
of the Empire as essential underpinnings of British identity;
and the Labour Party because, in the party's fledgling years
before the First World War, it supported the philosophy of
Irish nationalism in a well-meaning but essentially unthinking
and emotional manner, secure in the knowledge that the party
was in too minor a political position to have to do anything
meaningful about it.

Within a decade of Agar-Robartes moving his amendment, these political parties had substantially shifted their attitudes towards Ireland and their Irish allies. The Liberal Prime Ministers Asquith and Lloyd George despaired of resolving the Irish issue at a time when their major priority was meant to be bringing the war to a successful conclusion. Changing political fortunes throughout the war were of immense political significance – particularly the demise of constitutional nationalism in Ireland and its replacement by the radical revolutionary nationalism of Sinn Fein, allied to the collapse of the last exclusively Liberal government and the entry of the Conservatives into the wartime coalition from 1915. The consequent rise in influence for the Conservatives' allies, the Ulster unionists, meant that the pre-war relationships between the British political parties and their Irish allies underwent radical change. By the end of the war the last Liberal Prime Minister, Lloyd George, was at the head of a Tory-dominated coalition far more sympathetic to Ulster unionist concerns than the previous solely Liberal government of Asquith had ever been to Irish nationalists. As the constitutional Home Rulers were replaced by radical republicans who refused to take their seats in London in 1918, the Ulster unionists and their friends in the Conservative-Liberal coalition were in a far more influential position in Westminster than Irish nationalists had been at the beginning of the war. Lloyd George found himself at the head of a post-war British government now locked into a vicious military campaign with radical Irish separatists. After nearly forty years the accommodation between British Liberals and Irish nationalists (the latter supporting the former in return for the implementation of Home Rule) had certainly had its day.

By 1922 the traditional alliance between British Conservatism and Irish unionism was also reaching its conclusion. In the immediate post-war years British politics progressed from arcane discussion of Britishness and the Empire towards a more sophisticated debate on pressing social and economic issues. Apart from a minority of dogmatic ideologues, the Tories now had only a grudging sense of responsibility to their erstwhile allies in Ulster unionism that was far removed from the enthusiasm of the pre-war years. This had a lot to do with the fact that the Conservatives no longer needed to exploit Ulster unionist fears in order to propel themselves to power, as they now totally dominated Lloyd George's post-war coalition government.

Similarly, Labour's commitment to Irish nationalism (never more than lukewarm) faded rapidly when the excesses of militant Irish republicanism (particularly during the Irish Civil War) became apparent. The Labour leadership became acutely aware that sympathy with and support for Irish nationalist demands was hardly likely to be a vote winner amongst the British working class. Labour also had its previously unthinking emotional alliance with Irish nationalism severely challenged by the reality of being in government in 1924 for the first time and having to deal with the intricacies of the Irish Boundary Commission, established by the Anglo-Irish Treaty to determine the final course of the Irish border. Disillusionment with the (from a Labour perspective) irrational and unpredictable nature of Irish nationalism, and Irish politics in general, rapidly set in.

Finally, the Liberal Party had ceased to be a meaningful potential government after its catastrophic election defeat in 1924. Although Ireland was hardly the issue that brought the party down, it was one of many – including industrial unrest, women's suffrage and its inability to produce a satisfactory war strategy – which contributed to the impression that the party was overwhelmed and ill-equipped to function as a modern political machine. This was not helped by the great Liberal split between Lloyd George and Asquith in 1916, from which the party never recovered. Significantly, the Anglo-Irish controversy of the post-war years coincided with the most intense period of political instability in twentieth-century British history as the country moved in rapid succession from a two-party (Liberal and Conservative) political system to three-party politics and then, after 1924, back to a two-party system (this time Labour and Conservative).

It was this relentlessly negative experience of dealing with "the Irish Question" from 1912 to 1925 that led to the unspoken cross-party understanding that, once removed from the centre of British politics, Ireland should never be allowed to return. After all, Gladstone himself had said of the Irish issue that until it was solved "it will ride you like a nightmare. It will possess and absorb the public mind more and more, and the whole course of legislation will be impeded and obstructed".[1] The ambition of all British political parties to keep Ireland out of British politics was fulfilled over the next ninety years. Not even events as significant as the declaration of Irish neutrality in the Second World War, nor thirty years of communal violence in Northern Ireland – a part of the UK – in the late twentieth century in any way enticed successive British governments to get more involved in Irish affairs than they strictly had to.

Although, at various junctures throughout the twentieth century, the Conservative Party (or, usually, the traditionalist wing of the party) attempted to burnish their patriotic credentials by identifying with Ulster unionism, this faded as the century progressed. The embarrassment and bewilderment at Enoch Powell's espousal of unionism in the 1970s only served to illustrate the gulf that had developed between modern, meritocratic post-war Conservatism and its nostalgic, imperialist past. Similarly, the potential electoral danger of identifying too closely with radical Irish nationalism is today as much a threat to the current Labour Party leadership as it was to Ramsay MacDonald nearly a century ago.

Through the years, British political parties have merely

reflected the indifference and bewilderment that the British electorate have exhibited towards Irish politics. Apart from periodic bouts of outrage at IRA bombs exploding in British cities or British soldiers being killed in Northern Ireland or the financial cost of maintaining Northern Ireland in the UK, the British public have demonstrated a sustained bafflement and profound lack of interest in the complexities of Irish ethnic nationalism and, in particular, its complete irrelevance to mainstream British politics. In these circumstances, it is no wonder that most British politicians have sought to reflect the electorate's mood and distance themselves from reimmersion in these ethnic and religious disputes which, from a British perspective, often seemed to owe more to ancient history than to a sophisticated and modern political discourse. Undoubtedly, although it is rarely mentioned these days, the unwelcome reality of how Irish politics dominated British politics for more than two generations in the early twentieth century is buried deeply in the collective memory of the British political class.

Who would have predicted that in the early twenty-first century it would have been Britain's attempts to extricate itself from the European Union (EU) that resulted in Ireland – and, more specifically, the Irish border – reasserting itself at the centre of British politics once again? Given that "the Welsh Wizard" Lloyd George was meant to have solved the Irish problem in 1921, readers unfamiliar with Anglo-Irish politics may be puzzled as to why, nearly a century after the Irish Question was purportedly solved, the Irish border is rearing its head once again.

This is not a history of Anglo-Irish relations, or of the partition of Ireland. It is not even a history of the Irish border. But it does seek to explain, through an examination of their political forebears' experience a century ago, why contemporary British politicians preferred not to allow any consideration of Irish politics back into British politics if it could be at all avoided. Irrespective of the various interpretations as to why there is an Irish border in the first place – with Irish nationalists believing that the establishment of the border was an act of British perfidy sundering a natural geographic and cultural unit in order to further British party political advantage, and unionists arguing that the border is merely the recognition of the reality that the British population of north- eastern Ireland wished to retain its British identity particularly after Irish nationalism became more extreme and anti-British in the early twentieth century – the continued existence of a border in Ireland is undoubtedly controversial. Undeniably *all* borders are ridiculous to one extent or another. All of them in different respects have their own *Puckoon*-like qualities, as immortalised in Spike Milligan's comic novel on the Irish border in which a village and even houses are divided in half. Given, however, that once the existence of a border is decided upon and a line has to be demarcated somewhere, is the Irish border more ridiculous than, for example, the myriad of Belgian and Dutch enclaves encroaching on each other's territory along their joint border? The location of all borders – with the exception of obviously man-made borders such as those drawn in the Middle East after the First World War – inevitably has some ethnic, linguistic or historical basis in reality. The Irish border is no exception. But unlike most borders, and remarkably for one that has been in existence for nearly a century, the Irish border continues to provoke deep-seated emotions. The Brexit controversy has inevitably stoked these emotions further.

The Historical Background

Historically, the northern province of Ulster had always been regarded as separate from the rest of Ireland by both southerners as well as committed Ulster unionists. I remember my first introduction to this debate in the archaeology department at Queen's University Belfast. It was an issue of some historical controversy: was Ireland first settled from the south, directly from Iberia and western Europe, or did the first inhabitants enter into the north via Britain, specifically Scotland? The political ramifications of this were apparent to all concerned. In Irish mythology and subsequently Irish history and politics, debate still rages as to whether the northern hero Cuchulainn was an Irish hero or a defender of the north against the hordes from the south, as memorably commemorated in the famous pre-Christian Irish saga *The Cattle Raid of Cooley*. Cuchulainn's valour and sacrifice are claimed by republicans and loyalist paramilitaries with equal enthusiasm. The author Ian Adamson has even gone as far as to claim that the Scottish Protestant planters of Ulster who colonised the province in the seventeenth century were merely reclaiming the land abandoned after their ancestors left Ireland for Scotland a thousand years previously.

The pioneering Dutch geographer M V Heslinga adopted

an environmentally determinist approach when he argued that the subsequent separateness of Ulster was inevitable given the geographical barriers of mountains, impenetrable forests and in particular the remnants of the Ice Age landscape of drumlins, lakes, marshes and moraines all contributing to Ulster's physical, cultural and ultimately political isolation from the rest of Ireland. Utilising these natural features was the Black Pig's Dyke, a series of pre-historic earthworks reputedly marking the border between the ancient province of Ulster and the rest of Ireland.

Furthermore, although Ireland had cultural, linguistic and, specifically, religious unity particularly during the golden period of the Early Irish Church, it crucially lacked political unity. This was meant to be reflected in the role of the High King of Ireland, but this was largely an honorary symbol of Irish cultural rather than political unity. In reality, Ireland was divided into as many as 150 minor kingdoms; political instability was endemic. This instability led directly to the first English (or more specifically Norman) intervention in the twelfth century. Although the Normans and later centralising English kings rapidly extended their authority throughout most of Ireland, they failed to penetrate the northern Gaelic fastness of Ulster (apart from the Ards peninsula plus Carrickfergus and its castle).

Behind its geographical barriers, Ulster remained the most remote and Gaelic part of Ireland until (and even after) the new Tudor (and now Protestant) English nation-state under Henry VIII indicated its desire to impose thorough control on a half-subdued Ireland in order to prevent it falling into the clutches of its Catholic continental rivals Spain and France. However, it was only under Elizabeth I that Ulster began to fall to the English – but judicious exploitation of the province's geography through the skilful use of guerrilla tactics by the native Irish in Ulster meant that Gaelic Catholic Ulster was not defeated until the beginning of the seventeenth century. Even then, it was only open to Plantation – a process of colonising land that had been confiscated by Britain – by loyal Protestant settlers who hailed mostly, though not exclusively, from Scotland. Although the Ulster Gaelic chieftains had managed to maintain their virtual independence from central control in London through their inherent knowledge of the topography, Ulster was not immune from outside influence. The flow of settlers from Scotland in the past had long been a feature of Ulster settlement, although previously these immigrants had mainly been Catholic and Gaelic speaking themselves and thus integrated relatively easily into existing Ulster society.

The new arrivals were different. They were Presbyterians from Scotland and Anglicans from England and Wales. Over the next century, their numbers were regularly replenished from Britain to replace, on the more fertile land, the dispossessed native Irish now moved to the more marginal uplands.

The success of Plantation was not a foregone conclusion, and the rebellion of the dispossessed Catholic Irish in 1641 led to the deaths of many Protestants. This inculcated among Protestants an attitude of fear and suspicion of their Catholic neighbours which has arguably continued to the present. Eternal vigilance continued to be a characteristic of Ulster Protestantism even after Protestant supremacy was secured at the Siege of Derry and the Battle of the Boyne at the end of the century.

Although the Penal Laws in the eighteenth century were directed mainly against the Catholic population in Ireland, the non-conformist Presbyterian element in the Plantation of Ulster suffered also and this, allied to economic downturn, led to the migration of many Presbyterians (the Ulster Scots) to the American colonies. Their land in Ulster was, ironically, settled in turn by many Catholics moving up from the Irish midlands and southern borderlands of Ulster. This led to much sectarian aggravation, culminating in the founding in 1795 of the Orange Order to defend Protestant interests.

Ulster Presbyterians were also at the forefront of the United Irishmen – a secular republican movement seeking the complete separation of Ireland from Britain – in the 1790s and many were attracted by the republican philosophy of the new US and France. However, the Ulster Presbyterians were ultimately repelled by this new political philosophy as the theory of a democratic republican Ireland descended into sectarian bloodletting in the 1798 rebellion. Up till then Ireland had been theoretically independent of Britain, with its own Protestant-dominated parliament. However, the shock of the rebellion persuaded most Protestants to give up their parliament in Dublin through the Act of Union in 1800, in return for the UK guaranteeing Irish Protestants security and political preference in the reconfigured state.

The new dispensation seemed, from a Protestant perspective, to usher in a period of stability and prosperity. The Industrial Revolution developed the north-east of the country into a prosperous British industrial outpost in agrarian Ireland. But the Act of Union seemed to lead to the opposite in the rest of the country, with increased penury and poverty for many rural Catholics culminating in the famine of the mid-nineteenth century. Ulster *was* different. Its agrarian system brought over from Scotland, "the Ulster Custom", gave a modicum of security against eviction and enabled tenants to sell on their landholdings, a privilege unknown elsewhere in Ireland.

By the middle of the century Ireland, it seemed, had been integrated into the new state. Liberals and Conservatives contested parliamentary seats in Ireland just as they did elsewhere in the UK. In general, Liberals were elected in the south and Conservatives in the north. But all of this was about to change. The arrival of William Gladstone as Prime Minister in 1868, with his mission "to pacify Ireland", was seen by many unionists as a betrayal of the contract between themselves and the British government whereby they surrendered their Dublin parliament in 1800 in return for London guaranteeing their security. The disestablishment of the Church of Ireland in 1869, the passing of the first Land Act in 1870 and the establishment of the secret ballot in 1872 – resulting in the loss of Protestant landlords' influence over their tenants – caused anxiety particularly amongst the well-off Anglican ascendancy class. However, the birth of an aggressive and militant Irish nationalism in the 1870s led to the growth of an equally assertive Irish and then specifically Ulster unionism. It was the conflict between this nationalism and unionism that was to dominate both Irish and British politics over the next forty years.

The growth in the demand for Home Rule (limited self-government for Ireland inside the UK) and the Land Acts of the late nineteenth century appeared to Protestants to herald the reversal of the Protestant land confiscations of the seventeenth century and the imminent obliteration of Protestant political and social control of the country. All this revived the race memory of the 1641 rebellion – an attempted Catholic coup d'état – and other deep-seated, but not forgotten, assaults on the Protestant presence in Ireland, such as the Siege of Derry by the Catholic King James II in 1689 or the sectarian massacre of Protestants in the 1798 rebellion by the United Irishmen. From then on all Protestants, irrespective of their religious or class differences, began to cling together in the face of what they perceived as an aggressive and antagonistic reassertion of native Catholic Irish political power.

Ironically, it was the arrival of the Protestant Anglo-Irish landlord Charles Stewart Parnell as the new leader of the Irish Home Rule movement in 1880 that now presented the most severe challenge to his fellow Protestants. They now faced the most assertive and confident Catholic nationalist movement in Ireland since Daniel O'Connell and the Catholic Emancipation and Repeal campaigns in the first half of the nineteenth century. Known as "The Liberator", Daniel O'Connell was a charismatic populist leader who mobilised the demographic strength of the overwhelmingly Catholic population in Ireland to bring non-violent mass protest pressure on successive British governments in order to make Irish (and British) Catholics full and equal citizens in the UK. This was achieved in 1829. O'Connell sought to use the same tactics, unsuccessfully, to achieve a repeal of the Act of Union in the 1840s. In the late 1800s, Parnell was a new leader for the Home Rule movement to rally around; for the next forty years, Irish Protestants would attempt to counter the progress of this resurgent Irish nationalism as part of their campaign to remain citizens of the UK.

Creating the Irish Border

Gladstone's introduction of his First Home Rule Bill in 1886 saw the beginning of a forty-year period in which the Irish Question dominated British politics. Indeed, of all the pieces of legislation ever to come before the British parliament, the 1893 Second Home Rule Bill still holds the record for having the largest amount of parliamentary time spent on debating it. British parliamentary politics only escaped from this domination by Irish issues with the final approval of the course of the Irish boundary in 1925.

Although the first two Home Rule Bills were relatively easily defeated (the first in the House of Commons and the second in the House of Lords), Ireland's politics were irrevocably changed by them. The 1886 Bill was greeted by sectarian rioting, particularly in Belfast, and this was to become an increasingly depressing characteristic of northern politics over the next forty years. For the first time, British politicians mused about the steps required to solve increasing political and sectarian tensions, particularly in the north of Ireland. The Liberal imperialist Joseph Chamberlain, whose opposition to Gladstone's Irish policy split the Liberal Party in 1886, speculated about a federal Britain with a parliament at Belfast. This was to be based on the Canadian model in which distinctive

cultures (such as that of Quebec, or in this case Ulster) could
be recognised, and it was to be related to Chamberlain's even
more ambitious proposals for Imperial Federation across
the British Empire. Indeed, as early as 1833, Whig historian
and politician Lord Macaulay had remonstrated to Daniel
O'Connell during the debates over repealing the Act of
Union that O'Connell's arguments for a separate parliament at
Dublin could also be used to justify a parliament for Ulster in
the city of Londonderry, given its symbolism for Ulster Protestant identity dating back to the seventeenth century.

In the event, these Home Rule crises passed, and for the next
twenty years Ireland was ruled by a succession of Conservative governments intent on "killing Home Rule by kindness".[2]
This involved firm government allied to democratic, economic
and land reform, as well as state investment in infrastructure,
particularly in the impoverished west of Ireland. However,
unionist suspicions never went away; unionists remembered
that their Conservative allies had themselves endeavoured
to negotiate with Parnell in 1885. From then on, unionists in
Ireland began ultimately to rely on their own resources, establishing the Irish Unionist Alliance in 1891 in order to keep all
of Ireland out of the clutches of Home Rule.

Significantly, in a move which was to have great significance
during the debates on the Third Home Rule Bill, when not
only Ireland but Ulster itself was threatened by partition, 1905
saw the establishment of a separate Ulster Unionist Council

to represent the interests of Protestants in the north-east of Ireland, where they were far more numerous and concentrated. In Ulster, Protestants made up over fifty per cent of the population, whereas they accounted for less than ten per cent of the population in the other three Irish provinces, and most of them lived in Dublin. After Home Rule had been seen off in 1886, the general election that year resulted in seventeen Ulster Unionists being elected. There were a further nineteen southern unionists elected but, in an illustration of the now-closer links between the British Conservative Party and Irish unionism, all but two of them represented British mainland constituencies.

After the two general elections in 1910, the Liberal government became dependent upon Irish Home Rule MPs, while the following year's Parliament Act ended the Conservative-dominated House of Lords' veto on legislation. Irish unionism, after a nearly twenty-year hiatus, was once again in mortal danger. With a hostile government once more committed to Home Rule, unionists were now without effective allies.

Furthermore, the nature of the threat had intensified. The new assertive Irish nationalism they faced was "Irish Irelandism", a potent combination of cultural, economic and political nationalism which was to reach its apogee with the ascent of Sinn Fein after the First War. This was essentially a southern nationalist philosophy which asserted that the essence of Irishness – Gaelic and Catholic – was the polar opposite of what Irish (specifically Ulster) unionists cherished: their Britishness, the Empire, the monarchy and, above all, their Protestantism. To many Irish nationalists, Ulster Protestantism in particular was foreign and non-Irish, and they described Ulster dismissively as the "black north". This attitude was exemplified by future Governor-General of the Irish Free State and former Home Rule MP Tim Healy, who boasted that he "knew nothing whatever about Belfast". He said, "I only spent 24 hours there and they were the most unhappy 24 hours I have ever spent in my life".[3]

However, Ulster Protestants were fortunate in that Sir Edward Carson had become unionist leader in 1910 and Bonar Law, of Ulster Protestant background himself, had replaced Arthur Balfour as Conservative leader in 1911. Both Carson and Bonar Law believed that the threat of Home Rule would lead to the destruction of the UK and ultimately the entire British Empire. In addition, the Tories sensed a political opportunity. The Conservative Party regarded itself as the natural party of government, but by 1911 had been out of office for over five years. The party had lost the two most recent general elections, and had little prospect of winning one in the near future. Undoubtedly, in addition to their ideological affinity with the Irish unionists, the Conservatives knew that there was massive popular support in Britain for the predicament in which the Ulster unionists now found themselves. Equally, the Tories remembered that their adroit exploitation of British jingoism in the middle of the Boer War had resulted in their massive "khaki election" victory – one heavily influenced by wartime patriotism – in 1900, and they therefore hoped to propel themselves back into power by repeating that tactic, this time on the issue of Irish Home Rule.

Despite increasing political instability in Ireland from April 1912, when the Liberal Prime Minister Asquith introduced the Third Home Rule Bill that led to the establishment of two rival paramilitary armies in Ireland – one unionist and one nationalist, both importing arms from Germany – Ulster unionists did not demand the partition of Ireland and the establishment of an Irish border until late 1913. Prior to this, *all* British and Irish political parties had rejected the Agar-Robartes amendment of the previous year – the Liberals and Irish nationalists because they rejected any division of Ireland, and the Irish unionists because it would reduce their community in the south of Ireland to a rump state, separated as those unionists would be from the concentration of their co-religionists in the north-east. Even northern unionists rejected the amendment, as it proposed to save only four of the nine historic Ulster counties from absorption into a Catholic-dominated Home Rule Ireland.

Inside a year, all of this had changed. The Ulster unionists realised (and the southern unionists feared) that only the north (and not even all of that) could realistically be exempted from Home Rule. In the same way as Bonar Law had enthusiastically supported the unionists in their parliamentary (and extra-parliamentary) opposition to Home Rule, the Conservatives now also accepted that it was inevitable that Ireland would be divided politically. The question then was how this would be done. Asquith had tacitly admitted during the course of the parliamentary debates on Home Rule that ultimately "special provision" would have to be made to accommodate Ulster unionist opposition, but he was not prepared to indicate what that could be until Home Rule was on the statute book and had become the law of the land.

In the meantime, debate raged about exactly where the new Irish border should be. Initially it was accepted that this would not be an international border, as it would only be dividing areas which would both remain part of the UK. In addition, there was no proposal at this stage that the north of Ireland would become a self-governing entity itself, as it was envisaged that the part of Ireland excluded from the provisions of the proposed Home Rule Act would simply continue to be administered directly from Westminster.

Initially, Carson, as the unionist leader, proposed the exclusion of the entire nine-county historic province of Ulster from Home Rule. As a Dublin-born southern unionist, Carson was in a difficult ideological position, as were the British Tories. Their initial encouragement of Ulster unionist intransigence was a device to wreck the Home Rule proposal for all of Ireland. Now they both recognised pragmatically,

but realistically, that only that part of Ireland with a numerically strong Protestant population could be exempted. It was
then a question of maximising the number of Protestants to
be excluded while minimising the risk to the future viability of
the excluded area by limiting Catholics (and therefore nationalists) inside that area to a number that could be tolerated
from a security perspective.

It would have proven difficult if the entire province, with
more or less equal numbers of Catholics and Protestants, had
become the excluded area. This would have been easier to
achieve if London had remained responsible for security, but
it would have been far more difficult once it was agreed, five
years later, that a new Northern Ireland state was to be created,
responsible for its own security. Pragmatic Ulster unionists
realised that much of the historic province of Ulster and its
indigenous Protestant population, surrounded by an over-
whelming Catholic majority, would have to be abandoned to
the tender mercies of a nationalist-controlled Ireland. Given
that this was what Protestants feared the most, the abandonment of their co-religionists in the Catholic-dominated
Ulster border counties of Cavan, Donegal and Monaghan still
rankles a century on.

In the months before the outbreak of the First World War,
and just before Home Rule became law, the Liberal government finally indicated what "special provision" for Ulster
might consist of. Lloyd George had proposed on behalf of the

government in November 1913 that the four most unionist counties (Antrim, Down, Armagh and Londonderry) could be temporarily excluded from Home Rule for six years. In March 1914, his colleague Asquith suggested that each Ulster county plus the county boroughs of Belfast and Londonderry could individually vote on whether they wished to be excluded from the operation of the Home Rule Act for six years. This prompted an angry reaction from Carson, who said that for Ulster this amounted to a sentence of death with a stay of execution for six years. In addition, the unionists adamantly opposed local plebiscites or referenda, whether on a county basis or any other, as they knew that Home Rule would be accepted by not only Tyrone and Fermanagh with their Catholic majorities, but even by Catholic parts of the Protestant heartland such as South Down. Rejection of direct democracy was a feasible position to adopt in this pre-war period, although it would later become more difficult in the post-war era of the Treaty of Versailles and the new dispensation of "national self-determination", when plebiscites became all the rage in the Europe of the defeated empires.

In anticipation of getting immediate implementation of Home Rule in at least most of Ireland, nationalist leader John Redmond agreed in February 1914 to accept, temporarily, the exclusion of the six most Protestant counties of Ulster – despite the fact that two of them, Fermanagh and Tyrone, had nationalist majorities. At the same time, Bonar Law announced Tory support for the Ulster unionists' preferred option: the permanent exclusion of the same six counties. In effect, therefore, despite further attempted horse-trading at a meeting of party leaders including Carson and Redmond at Buckingham Palace in July 1914, this was the state of play on Ireland as the country headed for war.

Significantly, at the Buckingham Palace meeting Carson proposed that the excluded area should have administrative autonomy from the rest of the UK. This was the first time that unionists had suggested that Ulster should be run in any way differently to the rest of Britain. When Home Rule became law in September 1914, just after the outbreak of war – although its implementation was postponed for the duration of the conflict – both the Ulster unionists and their Conservative allies had already decided on their preferred option for the border between Ulster and the remainder of Ireland. Neither party deviated from this shared position from that date until the removal of the Irish issue from British politics through the ratification of the six-county border of Northern Ireland at the end of 1925. Their shared political objective from 1914 on was to save as much of Ulster as possible from the threat of a Home Rule parliament, remaining mindful of the fact that Asquith had guaranteed that there would be undefined amending legislation for Ulster at the end of the war.

This was almost the last direct involvement Asquith had in Ireland – apart from the 1916 Easter Rising – before he was removed as Prime Minister by Lloyd George and the Tories in December 1916. When, upon the outbreak of war, Bonar Law proposed national unity and the suspension of normal party politics for the duration of the conflict, Asquith breathed a sigh of relief. In his more optimistic utterances on Ireland he had stressed his belief that the granting of Home Rule was a concession large enough to keep Ireland quiet and to remove her from the centre of British public life. In his darker moments he suggested that British policy on Ireland should be to "submerge the whole lot of them, and their island, for say ten years, under the waves of the Atlantic".[4]

On the outbreak of the First World War, few people in Britain or Ireland would have been prepared to believe that only ten years later Ireland would be divided in two, with each part having its own parliament and an international border separating the island. This was not the inevitable outcome of the political turbulence in Ireland. The most significant factor, however, which determined the establishment of a border in Ireland was the constantly changing political developments in Britain and Ireland over the course of the war and, in particular, the fundamental change in the political balance of power in both countries. In fact, it could be argued that partition, and the appearance of an Irish border, was the least traumatic of many possible outcomes that could have easily involved bloody civil war and subsequent population transfers – which, ironically, would also have resulted in the same (or similar) partition and border. We should never forget that the events in late twentieth-century Yugoslavia had many echoes of early twentieth-century Ireland.

That there would soon be some sort of political border in Ireland was apparent when war broke out in August 1914. The issues to be resolved were where it was to be, when it would be implemented and whether it would be temporary or permanent. Once the Liberal government had given a commitment that there would be "special treatment" for Ulster at the conclusion of the war, and once the Conservative opposition and their Ulster unionist allies had agreed that their optimum demand was for the exclusion of six counties, it was only a question of when, not if. As the war progressed and the Conservatives as well as the unionist leader Carson entered the wartime coalition Cabinet in May 1915, followed in December 1916 by the overthrow of Asquith by Lloyd George supported by the Conservatives, it became obvious that the unionist position had strengthened while the nationalist position had weakened. The violence of the republican 1916 Easter Rising only made unionists even more determined to fight for partition – if they were previously unwilling to accept the blandishments of the moderate Home Rulers, they became even more obdurate when faced with the prospect of being ruled by the zealous republican dogmatists who replaced the Home Rulers in nationalist Ireland from 1917 on. Redmond and his party recognised that even though Home Rule was now the law of the land, potential power and patronage were rapidly leaching away from them. In desperation, they accepted Lloyd George's post-Rising offer of a wartime granting of Home Rule with a temporary exclusion for Carson's six counties. What Redmond failed to realise was that Lloyd George had at the same time indicated to Carson that the exclusion would be permanent. This, in effect, offered the Ulster unionists what they had wanted ever since 1911: the maximum area that they could control.

In the end, Lloyd George's machinations became academic, as the southern unionists, whose greatest fear was now isolation in a partitioned Catholic-dominated state rather than Home Rule itself, mobilised their influential Tory allies, particularly in the House of Lords. They persuasively argued that the granting of Home Rule so soon after the Easter Rising could be interpreted as a reward for treason. Lloyd George's plan thus remained stillborn, but it was significant that this was the first time both nationalists and unionists had agreed, however fleetingly, on Home Rule with six-county exclusion.

This was followed again in 1917 when, in order to assuage concerns in the US and British Dominions over the British government's Irish policy at this crucial period of the war, Lloyd George once more offered immediate Home Rule with six-county exclusion or, as an alternative, an Irish Convention charged with bringing forward an acceptable scheme of self-government. Lloyd George was particularly concerned about being able to demonstrate to a concerned wider world that the Irish themselves were determining their future rather than being informed what it should be by the imperial parliament. This latest proposal was again scuppered by the Ulster unionists, who were confident that they had already been promised what they wanted: permanent six-county exclusion.

At the end of the war in 1918, Lloyd George – fresh from his victory in the general election but now a Liberal Prime Minister at the head of a Conservative-dominated peacetime coalition government – had once more to contend with the intractability of Irish politics. As the new government wearily returned to the vexed subject, Liberal Cabinet minister Winston Churchill, who had supported Home Rule before the war, spoke for the entire Cabinet when he stated that with the Great War "every institution, almost, in the world was strained". He went on:

> Great empires have been overturned. The whole map of Europe has been changed... but as the deluge subsides and the waters fall we see the dreary steeples of Fermanagh and Tyrone emerging once again. The integrity of their quarrel is one of the few institutions that have been unaltered in the cataclysm which has swept the world.[5]

Some sort of Home Rule clearly had to be implemented as the 1914 Act was still on the statute book. Lloyd George had three options. His government could implement the original Act together with an enabling bill to exclude Ulster; it could repeal it; or it could supersede it with new legislation. Lloyd George chose the latter option and appointed Walter Long to chair the Cabinet committee on Ireland, which had been charged with seeking a way forward. In appointing Long, Lloyd George effectively acknowledged that any new policy must attract widespread Tory as well as unionist support. Long had been Chief Secretary for Ireland in the previous Conservative government, and chairman of the Irish Unionist Party MPs in the House of Commons from 1906 to 1910. His appointment was designed to guarantee the acquiescence of Tory back-benchers and to reassure southern unionists. By the time Long's committee had begun to meet, Home Rule was basically dead as a solution to the Irish problem; in the 1918 general election the Home Rulers had been replaced in Ireland by more ideo-logical republican separatists. Furthermore, the government was beginning to have to concentrate on a growing violent republican insurgency in Ireland. The 1920 Government of Ireland Act, which finally established the Irish border, was the ultimate outcome of the deliberations of Long's committee as well as being the direct descendant of the pre-war Third Home Rule Act. Given that rapid political change had occurred in both Britain and Ireland, in effect the Act dealt with the Irish problem as it was before rather than after the war.

In 1918, towards the end of the war, an earlier version of

Long's Cabinet committee had in fact begun to work within an ideological framework of federalism for the entire British Isles, foreshadowing the basic outlines of what was to become the Government of Ireland Act two years later. Following the Home Rule controversy, this had appeared to many intellectuals to be an attractive proposition which could potentially square the circle of preserving the unity of the UK whilst giving political recognition to the diversity inside it. This earlier 1918 committee proposed a Council of Ireland and exclusion for a six-county Ulster, subject to a plebiscite at the end of the war, together with a confirmatory referendum seven years afterwards.

This early version was rejected by the Cabinet, which believed it was inappropriate to consider such a radical constitutional realignment while the Irish situation was deteriorating so rapidly. In addition, many Conservatives also believed that federalism was being used as a convenient pragmatic device merely to extricate the government from its Irish difficulties. The Labour Party, however, despite its official policy of historically supporting traditional Home Rule, was supportive, and leading members such as J H Thomas (who was to become Labour's spokesman on Ireland) and Arthur Henderson began to suggest the application of the federal principle to the entire UK. They argued that federalism could be the answer to the dilemma of needing to preserve the Union while protecting both Ulster and southern Irish unionists and at the same time granting nationalist Ireland what could no longer be denied to them. However, Ulster unionists saw federalism as Home Rule by another name – and nationalist Ireland, by 1918, had advanced substantially from demanding traditional Home Rule. In the end, Lloyd George felt that it was more important, and pragmatically more desirable, to deal with the Irish Question directly and delay consideration of the larger issue of federalism. Long personally believed that the Cabinet had made a mistake in pushing a purely Irish solution rather than a more inclusive federal bill, but Lloyd George's political instincts proved to be correct: federalism was quietly dropped in mid-1918 when it became obvious that it had no mass support either in England or amongst Irish nationalists or unionists.

Nevertheless, the controversy over Ireland, and the debate as to whether that country's national aspirations could be accommodated within the confines of the UK as it was constituted at the beginning of the twentieth century, did stimulate a lengthy debate on the issue of federalism. It is difficult to appreciate at this remove the extent to which that debate took centre stage during this period. Many contemporary opinion formers and politicians from all parties believed that a federal reconstituting of the UK could provide a solution to the seemingly intractable problem of how to reconcile divergent national aspirations in Ireland. They were also convinced that devolution of power to Scotland and Wales could provide a readjustment of the constitutional equilibrium away from what they interpreted as the unhealthy centralism of power that had been allowed to develop inside the UK. Even though the arguments for federalism were fatally flawed by the fact that the populations of Scotland and Wales transparently did not have the same thirst for Home Rule as the Irish, the influence of the federalist argument can be traced in Lloyd George's proposed solution to the Irish problem in 1919 and 1920. Although the idea of federalism as a solution to the centrifugal forces endangering the integrity of the UK inevitably declined and collapsed after the decision to allow most of Ireland to leave the UK, it provided the philosophical underpinning for the Government of Ireland Act of 1920, which would establish Northern Ireland and lay the legislative foundation for the creation of the Irish border the following year.

In October 1919, Long's second Cabinet committee on Ireland agreed to propose separate parliaments for north and south, alongside a common council with powers for the whole island. The theory was that this would ultimately dovetail with the adoption of a federal system of government for the entire UK. Long's proposal was developed into an all-Ireland federal council whose powers could be granted if the two parliaments together agreed to delegate such authority. This theoretically could satisfy the pledge not to coerce or betray Ulster as well as guaranteeing British withdrawal from all of Ireland. From a British perspective this was an attractive proposition, as it would theoretically free Britain from the continuous immersion in Irish problems it had experienced over the previous forty years. The committee rejected calls for a plebiscite, echoing Balfour's criticism that Ireland should not be treated and carved up like a conquered central European state. Long also betrayed his southern unionist origins when he proposed a nine-county Ulster, as he saw this as ultimately facilitating reunification. The Ulster unionists, however, still committed to what from their perspective would be a viable northern political entity, only wanted six counties. The Cabinet, obviously preferring to have the unionists' support for the proposal, consequently backed down; in order to make the whole scheme work, the northern unionists had to be mollified.

The Government of Ireland Act establishing Northern Ireland became law in December 1920, with the new six-county state and the Irish border coming into existence on 3 May 1921. Lloyd George's main concern, given the Conservative domination of the coalition government, was to provide a solution to the Ulster question that would be congenial to the Tories and their allies, the Ulster unionists, before turning his skills towards negotiating a settlement for the rest of Ireland, where political instability and violence was now endemic. Undoubtedly, the passing of the Government of Ireland Act enabled Lloyd George to satisfy the Ulster unionists and his Conservative government allies prior to commencing negotiations with the resurgent (and far more strident than the

Home Rulers) Irish nationalists. In this he was assisted by the refusal of the newly elected Sinn Fein MPs to take their seats at Westminster, which meant nationalist Ireland had no input into the legislation nor into the parliamentary debate on the subsequent Anglo-Irish Treaty.

From a British perspective, the partition solution establishing two Irish parliaments theoretically took Ireland out of the realm of British politics, allowing Britain to withdraw from Ireland on her own terms. The theory was that because the Irish could now govern themselves, no Irish person could ever again complain about domination from Westminster. All Ireland was now autonomous, and ultimate reunification (a particular concern expressed by Britain's allies, the US and the Dominions) could be facilitated on an agreed basis in accordance with the topical principle of "self-determination" recently established by the Treaty of Versailles. Even with the benefit of a century of hindsight, it is difficult to imagine an alternative option to partition and the establishment of a border in Ireland that would have made sense from the British point of view, if their overriding concern was to withdraw from Ireland without coercing Ulster. If the Home Rulers rather than Sinn Fein had still been the dominant political force in the south, the Act would have been a brilliant solution. Previous Home Rule proposals in 1886, 1893 and 1912–14 had foundered on the rock of unionist opposition. Ironically, in 1920 the Fourth Home Rule Bill satisfied Ulster but not the extreme nationalists of Sinn Fein, who were the new masters in the south, where the Government of Ireland Act remained a dead letter amid escalating and relentless political violence. The Act, however, was the only one of the four Home Rule Bills to come into even partial effect. In this it reflected the new Tory-dominated balance of power at Westminster, but it is an irony that the only part of Ireland not wanting Home Rule was the only part to get it.

From a Conservative perspective it was obvious as early as 1917, if not before, that an Irish settlement involving some sort of Home Rule was essential to the war effort in order to attract the US into the war – and was probably an inevitable necessity to ensure the survival of the Empire after the war, given the concern and anxiety shown by the Dominions towards Britain's Irish policy. It is also apparent that Conservative support for the Ulster unionist case weakened between 1913 and 1918, undoubtedly because since 1916 the Conservatives had been the dominant partners in the wartime coalition government and there was no longer a need to "play the orange card", aligning with unionists in Ireland for political gain in the quest for office. Furthermore, as the Irish crisis intensified, it became increasingly obvious to both parties that although their short-term interests might coincide, the Conservatives were ultimately concerned about the future post-war welfare of the UK as a whole, whereas the Ulster unionists' overriding concern was for their own identity in Ireland.

Labour Party attitudes to Ireland were also changing. Prior to and even after the war, the Labour Party had provided general, vague and unthinking support for the political demands of moderate Irish nationalism. It became clear, however, that if the Labour Party aspired to become the governing party in the British state, then it had to distance itself from the revolutionary politics which had rapidly come to dominate Irish nationalism since 1918. Unlike the Conservatives, the Labour Party had no political debts to pay in Ireland. There had never been a cohesive and logically planned Irish policy in the Labour Party. For historical reasons, nearly all of the party (except in Belfast) had a deep and genuinely held emotional attachment to the moderate policies of the Home Rulers. Labour shared the Home Rulers' abhorrence of partition as a threat to the territorial integrity of Ireland. Consequently, Labour opposition to the Government of Ireland Act provided certainty at a time when its own policies on Ireland were in a state of flux, as it was increasingly criticised for slavishly following the traditional Home Rule policy when it was obvious that mainstream political demands in nationalist Ireland had moved well beyond that. Inevitably the party's cautious constitutionalism and parliamentarianism began to be threatened by its more radical members and some (though not a majority) of its Irish voters in Britain, who demanded direct action and a closer identification with the extra-parliamentary nationalism of Sinn Fein.

The Irish border demarcating the six counties of Northern Ireland from the rest of the country became a reality on 3 May 1921. Ironically, it first of all separated a Home Rule Northern Ireland from the bulk of the island that was still run directly from Westminster. Initially, Ulster unionists had been suspicious about the offer of a separate parliament in Belfast, fearing that it was some sort of dastardly ploy to detach them from the rest of the UK by treating them as semi-detached members who at some stage in the future could be delivered into the jaws of an all-Ireland state. They quickly warmed to the idea, however, when they saw that a separate parliament for Ulster permanently controlled by unionists and in charge of their security gave them added insurance against peremptory expulsion from the UK in the future. From then on, all the political energies of the unionists would be directed into maintaining the border that had come into existence that spring.

Consolidating the Irish Border

An important issue dividing and defining the British political parties before and during the First World War, Ireland began to fade into the background in the post-war years. It had previously dominated party politics on the floor of the House of Commons since 1886; now, after the upheaval of the war, it assumed the appearance of an irritation that was wearisome, but still likely to rear up and suddenly disrupt the predictability of British party politics. However, it was a problem that had remained unresolved for years, and now really needed to be laid to rest.

There was a new political spirit in post-war Britain as all parties began to become more involved with social and economic concerns, and so began to move away from fixation with the rights and wrongs of the competing nationalisms in Ireland. Although there had been popular support for the Ulster unionists in Britain in the pre-war years, that support did not endure or survive in the post-war years except amongst the right wing of the Conservative Party. There was no permanent constituency in Britain ready to defend Ulster's interests in equivalence to the Irish-American lobby in support of nationalist Ireland. Ulster unionists began to be perceived even amongst their erstwhile supporters as obdurate and stubborn, unwilling to compromise in the interests of the greater good and constantly whinging and grasping for more financial support from the British exchequer.

In Britain politics moved on; in Ireland they stayed the same. There developed a new sense of British identity which increasingly revolved around Anglocentrism and an anxiety to adapt the Empire into a Commonwealth, as befitted the rapidly changing political and social landscape of the inter-war years. The Irish conundrum was increasingly considered an obsolescent issue in British politics, albeit one with continued potential to cause political embarrassment and turbulence. However, the example of the Treaty of Versailles, stressing as it did the importance of "national self-determination", made it imperative to find a solution to the Irish Question and therefore, in 1920 and 1921, first the Ulster unionists and then the Irish republicans were manoeuvred into positions where compromise was deemed to be more acceptable than outright victory. That this proved to be possible was the result of a combination of coalition politics in immediate post-war Britain plus a major shift in British public opinion which demanded that Ireland finally be placed outside the realm of British party politics.

The continuation of the wartime coalition arrangement into peacetime British politics undoubtedly facilitated the government's attempts to solve the Irish problem in 1920–21. It enabled Lloyd George, the Liberal Prime Minister at the

head of a government
far the largest party,
anxieties by establish
through the Govern
ultimate aim, para
Ireland with a sep
closest ties to Grea
guarantee that it would not be
an all-Ireland system of government.

It was only after Ulster (and the Conservative Party,
reassured by the Government of Ireland Act that Lloyd George
was able to deal with militant republicans in the south. The
southern negotiators, led by Michael Collins, were adamant
that the agreement with Lloyd George in 1921 (the Anglo-
Irish Treaty) should supersede the previous year's Government
of Ireland Act in the same way as that Act had replaced the
pre-war Home Rule legislation. Ulster unionists were adamant
that this was not their understanding; the Anglo-Irish Treaty,
with its introduction of a Boundary Commission which
could potentially amend the border, threatened the viability
of Northern Ireland in a way that the Government of Ireland
Act did not. "What we have we hold," said Northern Ireland's
Prime Minister, the unionist Sir James Craig, asserting the
unionists' commitment to the Government of Ireland Act.
The Act had not only established the panoply of a separate leg-
islature in Northern Ireland but had also established a border

...nists, was now inviolate. To the unionists it ...glo-Irish Treaty which had created partition; it ...een created the year before by the Government ...Act.

...urther irony was that the Anglo-Irish Treaty was also ...sed to facilitate the future unification of Ireland, creating ...t did one government for the Irish Free State, a Dominion ...f the British Commonwealth (including the six previously excluded counties). However, it temporarily suspended the new government's jurisdiction over Northern Ireland and allowed the Ulster parliament to permanently exclude itself from the new Irish Free State – a choice that it took. After this self-exclusion, the terms of the 1920 Act remained in force in the now permanently excluded area. These terms included more restrictive financial provisions for Northern Ireland than it would have enjoyed as part of the Irish Free State, which had been granted fiscal independence by the Treaty – so there had been a very real financial inducement for the unionists to join a united Ireland. Furthermore, Northern Ireland's decision to exclude itself from the Irish Free State triggered the establishment of a Boundary Commission to determine the permanent course of the Irish border "in accordance with the wishes of the inhabitants, so far as may be compatible with economic and geographic conditions".[7] The presence of Conservative ministers – upholders of Ulster unionist interests – in Lloyd George's coalition government and as signatories of the

Anglo-Irish Treaty was meant to enable Ireland to be finally defused as a potent issue in British politics. The Conservatives were in a strategic position to ensure that Lloyd George had to take into account unionist fears and susceptibilities when negotiating with the representatives of advanced Irish nationalism. The Conservative leadership was also, by and large, able to keep its diehard pro-unionist element in check and to stop it sabotaging any potential accommodation to be arrived at between the government and Sinn Fein.

Notwithstanding this, the Boundary Commission provision in the Anglo-Irish Treaty caused immediate consternation amongst all unionists and many Conservatives. The Treaty did not specify whether the Commission would have the ability to make only minor adjustments to the new border, or whether it would be able to transfer sufficient swathes of Northern Ireland to the new Free State, thus making partition unviable and reunification inevitable. The central issue of the Anglo-Irish Treaty – the relationship of nationalist Ireland to the UK – was replaced by a new controversy over the future of the Irish border, despite the fact that the very existence of the Boundary Commission clause in the Treaty was a tacit acceptance of the fact that a separate and already established Northern Ireland would be able to exercise its right to opt out of a united Ireland. In reality, the Boundary Commission proposal posed no real threat to the Ulster unionists, despite the consternation it caused. It was understandable that the

Boundary Commission element should cause such (ultimately misplaced) anxiety to unionists, but the furore it led to over-shadowed the fact that in the negotiations nationalist Ireland had been presented with a fait accompli.

With Northern Ireland already in possession of a functioning parliament, government and security apparatus, the position of Protestant Ulster had already been secured by the time the fate of the rest of the country was decided. During the Treaty negotiations, the representatives negotiating on behalf of the doctrinaire republicans of Sinn Fein considered the principle of independence from Westminster and total Irish sovereignty to be more important than the supposedly temporary exclusion of the six north-eastern counties. This position would ultimately lead to the Irish Civil War after the Treaty was agreed.

In fact, Sinn Fein had already implicitly accepted partition by arguing that the state of Northern Ireland should be subservient to Dublin rather than London. Once again, the Ulster unionists refused to accept either an all-Ireland solution or a reduction in the size of the Northern Ireland state. Bonar Law stepped down as Conservative Party leader in October 1921, ostensibly due to ill health – but Conservative uneasiness on the likely terms of the Anglo-Irish Treaty was conjectured to be the real reason, as Bonar Law did not wish to be tainted by accusations of betraying Ulster. Despite Tory unease with the terms of the treaty and particularly the provision for the

Boundary Commission, leading Tories judged that the time was right for Ireland to finally be removed from British politics. Elements of the Tory press even urged Ulster to make some concessions towards Irish unity in the interests of peace, but the unionists refused to budge.

Prominent Tories such as Bonar Law and Stanley Baldwin were later relieved that the coalition government had produced the Treaty, as it meant that there was no going back to the uncertainty of the immediate post-war years. However, they kept these sentiments quiet at the time, fearing that they might be associated with the alleged betrayal of Ulster. Initially, Lloyd George was fêted for his achievement in solving the Irish problem – or, in A J P Taylor's evocative phrase, having "conjured it out of existence".[8] In 1923, the Speaker of the House of Commons ruled that discussion of Irish affairs in parliament would henceforth be out of order. It seemed that after forty enervating years the British parliament was about to be free of the Irish incubus. However, the central issue of Anglo-Irish relations, namely the status of Ulster and the future of the Irish border, refused to disappear.

The problem in 1924, as the Boundary Commission controversy began to escalate, remained the same as it had been in 1921 or 1914: because the future of Northern Ireland had merely been postponed by the Anglo-Irish Treaty and not settled, it returned to haunt British politics. The Treaty, when it was signed in 1921, was regarded as the crowning achievement of not only Lloyd George but the entire coalition government. Lloyd George could claim to have succeeded where Pitt, Peel and Gladstone had failed and Palmerston and Disraeli had not even tried. A year later, the unresolved Irish issue contributed to the end of Lloyd George's career as the Tories increasingly regarded him as erratic, corrupt and untrustworthy, with Stanley Baldwin damning the Prime Minister as "a dynamic force" who had destroyed his own party and would likely do the same to the Conservatives unless they escaped his coalition government.

The controversy over the Boundary Commission came at exactly the same time as one of the most politically turbulent periods in British political history. Tory criticism of the Treaty provisions as they affected Ulster extended to those Conservative ministers in the coalition government, such as Austen Chamberlain and Lord Birkenhead as well as Churchill. The diehard traditionalists – who objected strongly to what they saw as the appeasement of republican murderers and, in particular, to the financial and boundary clauses in the Treaty which they believed had betrayed Ulster – were relentlessly unforgiving of their former Tory colleagues who had served in Lloyd George's coalition, especially when Chamberlain admitted that the partition of Ireland "was a compromise, and like all compromises is illogical and indefensible".[9] Although the diehard element in the Conservative Party was not by now as influential as it had once been, it is undeniable that the Treaty "betrayal", which most diehards regarded as an unacceptable placation of the enemies of the British Empire, lent renewed impetus to the right wing and led to the rejection of not only Lloyd George but also their own leaders in the coalition. This all happened at a time when the new Conservative leader, Stanley Baldwin, was attempting to reunite his party after the traumas of the coalition experience. For a time it seemed that the Tories would split on the one remaining issue of the Irish Question – the future of the Irish border.

The period between 1922 and 1924 saw three general elections and four governments. By the end of this upheaval, despite Lloyd George hoping to return to the centre of British politics, Ramsay MacDonald and Stanley Baldwin had restored two-party politics – comprising Labour and Conservative, respectively – after the chaos of three political parties all vying for power. In doing so they were determined that the lingering uncertainty over Ireland, which they believed had contributed substantially to that chaos, should be removed permanently from British politics. Neither Baldwin nor MacDonald were particularly interested in Ireland and did not want the Irish issue with all its unpredictability to explode again. Even so, it took another year for that to happen, after the Boundary Commission controversy was finally resolved in late 1925 by removing the outstanding inducements for Irish unity which so threatened Northern Ireland. Indeed, Ireland continued to send ripples through British politics well into the mid-1920s and beyond. According to Churchill, the Anglo-Irish Treaty and its aftermath paved the way for the "Baldwin-MacDonald Regime" that persisted well into the late 1930s. The manner of the final settling of the Irish Question vindicated the doctrine of appeasement for a generation of politicians who came of age in the inter-war years. The irony was that some Tories regarded Churchill himself, who would later become known as the great anti-appeaser of the 1930s, as one of the arch-appeasers on the Anglo-Irish Treaty.

The political demise of Lloyd George in 1922, when the Conservatives abandoned the coalition, meant that the author of both the Government of Ireland Act and the Anglo-Irish Treaty was no longer at the centre of political power in Britain. Both measures were intended ultimately to bring about a united Ireland and the abolition of the border – although many Irish nationalists failed to interpret the situation in this way at the time. Subsequent holders of the Prime Ministerial office – Bonar Law, Stanley Baldwin and Ramsay MacDonald – did not share Lloyd George's ultimate ambition of Irish reunification. Paramount to them was the necessity of removing all traces of the Irish problem from the centre of British political life. It was ironic that after Lloyd George's demise it was Bonar Law and the anti-Treaty Tories who had to implement the Treaty after 1922.

In the period between 1922 and 1925 all three Prime Ministers, suspicious of the continued propensity of Ireland to create havoc in British politics, embarked upon a policy of delay and obfuscation, particularly on the constitution of the Boundary Commission, as they were all aware of the combustible sensitivity of this issue in particular. Bonar Law also changed the financial clauses in the Treaty to make them less onerous on Northern Ireland. He was so determined to prevent the coercion of Northern Ireland that he was prepared to allow the rest of the country to become a republic if this would prevent such coercion. The net effect was to undermine those aspects of the Treaty that were meant to facilitate eventual Irish reunification. These delaying tactics were also exacerbated by the Northern Ireland government's outright refusal, in defiance of the terms of the Treaty, to nominate its boundary commissioner. The Irish Civil War of 1922–23, fought over acceptance or rejection of the terms of the Treaty, prevented the Irish Free State demanding the implementation of the Boundary Commission. Furthermore, the continued political violence south of the border was hardly a recommendation for the suitability of a state that could not control all of its own territory taking over that of its neighbour as well.

Baldwin's inertia, in particular, was facilitated by the disarray within Irish nationalism. The Irish Civil War not only split former republican comrades in the south but also divided northern nationalists to a perhaps even greater – although not as murderous – extent. In addition to the division between the pro- and anti-Treaty elements of nationalism, there was a split between the old Irish Nationalist Party, which was still electorally strong in the north, and Sinn Fein. Finally, there was a difference in outlook between border nationalists optimistic about transfer to the Free State under the Boundary Commission recommendations and urban nationalists in Belfast who realised that no matter what recommendations the Boundary Commission might make they would be remaining in Northern Ireland.

In 1924 the Irish Free State, once more in full control of its territory after defeating the anti-Treaty republicans in the Irish Civil War, demanded that Britain's new Labour government finally constitute the Boundary Commission. However, Sir James Craig's refusal once more to appoint a northern commissioner caused anxiety in Westminster at the prospect of Ireland returning to the centre of British political life. Legislation amending the original Irish Free State Agreement Act, which gave the force of law to the Anglo-Irish Treaty, would now have to be rushed through parliament in order to allow MacDonald's government to appoint a commissioner on behalf of Northern Ireland. This ran the risk of reopening the whole debate on the alleged betrayal of Ulster, especially in the Conservative-dominated House of Lords, with its residual sympathy for the plucky Ulster unionists in their opposition to the forces of republican darkness. Baldwin feared that any Labour attempt to bypass Northern Ireland would be likely to be thrown out by the Tory Lords, in which case, according to

Deputy Cabinet Secretary Thomas Jones, "Ireland would be back in our politics".[10]

Baldwin was aware, and Lloyd George even more so, of the dangers and opportunities presented by a general election being fought on a Lords-versus-Commons basis, which would be a repeat of the 1910 "people or peers" general elections, and could provide a reunited Liberal Party with the opportunity to make a political comeback. Lloyd George still regarded the Anglo-Irish Treaty as his crowning achievement, and saw this latest controversy over the Boundary Commission as providing a chance for him to return to front-line politics. MacDonald, for his part, did not wish to afford Lloyd George the opportunity of once again rivalling Labour, given the serious effort the Labour leader had put into assiduously building up Labour's credibility as the progressive alternative to the fading Liberals. In fact, Macdonald's cautious – not to say legalistic – progress on implementing the Boundary Commission aspect of the Treaty was a classic example of his overriding concern with refuting Churchill's withering dismissal of Labour as not "fit to govern".[11]

In the event, Baldwin managed to prevail upon his diehards (or sufficient numbers of them) not to vote down MacDonald's amending legislation, the approval of which enabled the Boundary Commission to be established and carry out its work over the course of the next year. That the Conservatives decided not to play the "orange card" showed how far they had come over the previous decade. It also illustrated the febrile nature of British party politics in the mid-1920s, as Baldwin, a cautious politician at the best of times, was acutely conscious of the possibility that Conservative support for the Ulster unionists would merely facilitate Lloyd George's return to power at the subsequent general election.

Instead, the Conservatives fought the 1924 general election on "the red card of anti-socialism", castigating the Labour government for its links to Soviet Russia. The outcome of this election was a Tory majority of 211 – the largest government majority in early-twentieth-century British politics. This ushered in a period of thirteen years in which Stanley Baldwin became the dominant British politician of his generation. It also ended the domination of Irish affairs in the British parliament as, with such a majority, Baldwin could more or less do what he wanted, whether on Ireland or any other issue. Furthermore, it meant that the Liberals, with only forty MPs remaining, faced the end of their existence as a meaningful political party.

Paradoxically, it was an election result that was not entirely uncongenial to Labour. An election fought on Lords-versus-Commons lines on the Irish issue *might* have resulted in a Labour victory, but it ran the risk of benefitting the Liberals more than Labour. An election based on class lines might in the short term be (as it was) to Labour's disadvantage – but both the Tories and Labour wanted to see a return to a two-party system based on post-war class politics, rather than one based on irrational, unpredictable and potentially combustible issues such as Ireland. The latter ran the risk of encouraging a Liberal comeback, redolent as it was of the politics of the pre-war era when the Liberals were in their pomp. It is interesting to speculate what would have been the subsequent course of British politics if Ireland and the power of the House of Lords had been the main issues in the 1924 general election instead of socialism and Russia. One thing is obvious: neither Baldwin nor MacDonald wanted to take that risk.

There was one more postscript before Ireland and the Irish border were finally removed from British – or, more specifically, Westminster – politics. Although all the preparation involved in establishing the Boundary Commission had taken place during Labour's short period in office as a minority government, which ended in November 1924, the Boundary Commission met for the first time later that month, shortly after Baldwin's Conservative administration had replaced Labour. It spent most of the following year travelling around Northern Ireland receiving submissions. In November 1925, the Conservative *Morning Post* newspaper published what it purported to be the final recommendation of the Boundary Commission. It was clear from the *Morning Post* article that the Commissioners believed their duty was to determine the course of the border, not to decide whether there should be a border or not. Not only was there no suggestion that large areas of Northern Ireland should be transferred to the Irish Free State to the extent that the northern state would become unviable, but the recommendation was, in essence, that the border should remain as it was originally demarcated in the Government of Ireland Act five years previously – with a net gain of twenty-five thousand Catholics for the south and two thousand Protestants for the north. However, the real shock and embarrassment to the Free State was that it was expected to relinquish prosperous and Protestant East Donegal for impoverished and Catholic South Armagh. From a nationalist ideological and political perspective, the new state could not countenance the return to colonial control of liberated territory whose freedom had been won so recently and at such a price. The Free State had never considered the possibility that its territory would be handed back to the north. The south had always regarded the Boundary Commission as a device for, if not leading to the reunification of Ireland, at least bringing as many Catholics as possible inside the Free State's jurisdiction. Clearly Ulster unionists and many Conservatives had feared this transfer of northern territory back to the south; that is why they had been so angry with Lloyd George and those coalition Tories who had signed a treaty that included a clause which, as they saw it, threatened to surrender unionists to the mercies of the Free State.

It was clear to both the British and Irish Free State governments that, if the *Morning Post* report were proven to be correct, it would likely result in the collapse of the government in the south and its replacement with an anti-Treaty republican-Labour coalition. The consequences of this were as apparent to Baldwin's Conservative government as they had been for its Labour predecessor. Consequently, both Irish leaders were summoned to London where, on 3 December 1925, it was agreed that the Boundary Commission report would be shelved (which it was until 1969) and the existing boundary recognised. In return, the Free State was absolved of its responsibility under Article 5 of the Anglo-Irish Treaty to pay the British exchequer ten million pounds a year as its share of the British national debt. In addition, the proposed Council of Ireland, which had been designed with ingenuity by Lloyd George a mere four years previously in order to facilitate Irish reunification, was dissolved.

The outcome of this Tripartite Agreement was the Ireland (Confirmation of Agreement) Bill, which was considered by the House of Commons on 8 December 1925 – almost four years to the day after the signing of the Anglo-Irish Treaty. Baldwin was acutely conscious of the danger of the unresolved Irish issue returning to British politics. His overriding concern was that, if the Tripartite Agreement to confirm the existing boundary were rejected, and the Boundary Commission report were published, the Northern Ireland Prime Minister, Craig, might appeal to Conservative backbenchers on any of the outstanding issues that still concerned the unionists. The threat for Baldwin was that, even though the influence of the diehards inside the Tory party was not as strong as it had once been, a substantial number of Tory MPs still felt they had a residual obligation to Ulster unionists – and this might override their loyalty to their own party leader.

The danger was less, however, than it had been the previous year, when all three main political parties were balanced relatively evenly in the House of Commons. The divisions in the Conservative Party over the Treaty, and over the level of loyalty to be shown to Ulster unionism, could have split the party in 1922 or 1923 if the boundary crisis had taken place then. An unpredictable general election result in 1924 on the issue of Ireland might have cost Baldwin the leadership of his party as well as energising Lloyd George and reviving a reunited Liberal Party. By 1925, however, emotions had calmed and Baldwin had a much larger majority, which he could use to face down any opposition on Ireland. The scale of Baldwin's election victory meant that, in reality, he could determine the ultimate outcome of the Boundary Commission, as he faced no meaningful opposition from Labour, certainly none from the Liberals and, in truth, even less now from his own party.

Labour did not have to concern itself with a similar potential party split over Ireland; its militant wing in support of advanced Irish nationalism was vocal, but neither influential nor very large. Even so, it was with relief that Labour welcomed the Tripartite Agreement as it ensured that no future Labour government would find itself reimmersed in the unresolved Irish morass (until 1969, when the troops went into Northern Ireland). The Liberal Party also welcomed the agreement for the same reasons, but by 1925 Liberal Party policy on Ireland was irrelevant as it was not expected that the party would ever again be in a position to form a government. In terms of pragmatic politics, it was now in all the parties' strategic interests for the status quo to be accepted. Even Craig realised that the outcome had provided the stability and permanence which he and his Ulster unionists had been pressing for over the previous ten years. In the event, the legislation was passed.

On 8 December 1925, after forty years, Ireland ceased to be a dominating political influence in Britain. The transfer of responsibility for Irish affairs from London to Dublin and Belfast, with a 310-mile border separating the two, meant that Ireland was now removed from its pivotal position in British politics for the first time since the Act of Union in 1800.

Don't Mention the Irish Border

Following the British parliament's approval of the Tripartite Agreement, which buried the Boundary Commission's recommendations and confirmed the course of the Irish border as outlined in the Government of Ireland Act of 1920, the Irish border was permanently established – and it has existed ever since. In truth, since at least 1913 the partition of Ireland had seemed the most likely outcome of the conflict between the two competing nationalisms on the island of Ireland. However, in the subsequent twelve years the bewildering interpretation of where the border would be drawn had remained unresolved. In that time it had moved confusingly from encompassing the entire nine counties of Ulster to only four of these counties, and then back to six. There were other imponderables as well. How temporary or permanent was the border going to be? Was it always going to be based on the county boundaries, or on the boundaries of smaller administrative areas such as District Electoral Divisions or Poor Law Unions? Were the people to be affected going to be asked for their views, or was the line of the border going to be imposed from above?

This uncertainty over such a long period of time increased political instability in Westminster as well as Ireland. Initially, the Irish border was intended as an internal one inside the

United Kingdom of Great Britain and Ireland, following as it did the county boundaries previously established over three hundred years. It then became a boundary between Britain and one of her Dominions, when the Irish Free State was established in 1922. It became an economic frontier when the Free State set up a customs barrier in 1923. It then became a truly international boundary when Ireland cut off all former colonial ties with the British Commonwealth in 1948.

Although the border's security sensitivity was heightened during both the Irish Republican Army (IRA) Border Campaign of 1956–62 and the much longer "Troubles" between 1968 and 1998, its economic significance was reduced when both the Republic of Ireland and the UK joined the European Economic Community (EEC) in 1973. Renewed economic disruption resulted from the abandonment of currency parity between the Irish punt and the British pound in 1979, while Ireland's adoption of the euro in 2002 created a volatile shopping and trading zone along the border. Smuggling became endemic at times when the availability of goods, or the duties being charged on them, varied between the two sides of the border. Such periods included the Economic War between Britain and Ireland in the 1930s; the Second World War, with its rationing; and the 1980s, when EU duties or grants on the export of livestock differed between the two parts of Ireland, leading to the smuggling of farm animals. The smuggling of goods for personal use largely ended by the 1970s, as restrictions were withdrawn, personal entitlements were increased and travel across the border became much harder as a result of increased security.

The launch in 1993 of the European Single Market– designed to abolish internal border controls on the movement of capital, goods, services and citizens – intended that economic conflict across the Irish border and between Ireland and Britain would be dissolved into a wider European constellation of regions – albeit, paradoxically, at a time of violent political conflict and a more militarised border zone in Ireland. The south would have liked to have also joined the Schengen arrangements on unimpeded travel in the EU, but could not do so as it would have disrupted the post-1923 Common Travel Area with Britain, which opposed joining Schengen. One country joining without the other would have led to an external EU frontier on the Irish border, with increased security and border checks.

Ironically, that is what may now happen if the Irish border becomes not only an international border but, for the first time, the western land border of the EU. Notwithstanding this, the border is essentially open, allowing free passage of people since 1923 and of goods since 1993. The current concern is that if Britain and Ireland move to different customs regimes, and Ireland remains in the European Single Market as Britain exits from it, there will be a reimposition of border controls with all the possible political and military implications of this.

The underlying fact that the partition of Ireland was also the partition of the UK did not seem to trouble the British government or people. In losing one-fifth of its territory after the First World War, the victorious UK lost a larger proportion of its territory than did the defeated Germany. However, there was no irredentist movement in Britain for the recovery of the south of Ireland. The Irish Question had been answered, and so it faded out of the sphere of British domestic politics. The palpable relief at that time that Ireland was off the British agenda was matched only by an equal measure of perplexity when it reappeared half a century later at the beginning of the Northern Ireland conflict.

The partition of Ireland through the establishment of an Irish border was not simply a landmark in the history of Ireland but a formative event in the history of the modern UK. Partition created not two Irelands, but one and a half Irelands. The north-east of the island would not move to full independence from Britain, but equally it was never totally viewed by the rest of the UK as being an integral part of that state. Conversely, most English people, because of indifference or ignorance rather than malevolence, don't regard Ireland as foreign, let alone an independent state. This, not surprisingly, irritates Irish people immensely. Partition, from Britain's perspective, brought half a century of peace and relief in which it gave no thought to Ireland – until the conflict re-emerged, first with the Troubles and now with Brexit. Once more, the Irish border today sits immovably and apparently insolubly as the central issue in the relationship between Britain and Ireland.

The centrifugal political forces that culminated in the partition of Ireland also began a process which transformed both Ireland and Britain from being strongly centralised countries to having a much more devolved form of politics. Although in the early twentieth century federalism had been rejected as the political way forward for the United Kingdom of Great Britain and Ireland as a whole, it had in essence become the basis of the modern UK by the end of the twentieth century. This federalist influence could be seen firstly in the creation of Northern Ireland, and secondly in the granting of devolved responsibilities to both Scotland and Wales nearly eighty years later. Ireland had also been administered in a strongly centralised fashion, albeit with its own Viceroy and a Chief Secretary who sat in the British Cabinet.

Inevitably, after partition, north and south moved further apart. It is interesting to note that the use of Irish national emblems such as the shamrock and the harp featured extensively in the late-nineteenth-century campaigns against Home Rule: in the minds of Irish unionists then, at least, there was no overt contradiction between being both British and Irish at the same time. But by the time of the Third Home Rule Bill these displays had disappeared from unionist propaganda and were considered exclusively nationalist symbols by people in the new Northern Ireland. Equally, in the new Free State, which was ninety-five per cent religiously homogenous, it was easier to develop a functioning nationalist society (which was difficult enough for an impoverished small state emerging from a vicious internecine civil war) than to put energies into attracting and accommodating people in Northern Ireland, a fractious but substantial minority, when there was every expectation that a successful outcome to this effort could not be guaranteed. A similar attitude took hold in Northern Ireland where, after mobilising Protestant fears and prejudices, the new northern government was either unwilling or unable (or both) to offer the hand of conciliation to the resentful but substantial Catholic minority. Northern Ireland thus truly became, in Craig's words, "a Protestant Parliament and a Protestant State".[12]

All British parties accepted the new political dispensation. Ireland, north and south, was now out of sight and out of mind. British politicians intended to keep it this way – indeed, they welcomed this new relationship to Ireland even when it was obvious that the changed order had disadvantaged them. For example, it is undeniable that the loss of so many Irish nationalist MPs in 1922 must have accelerated the Liberal Party's decline, given that it removed one side of the progressive political axis of Liberal, Labour and Irish nationalists while politically helping Labour in terms of electoral support. Irish voters in Britain no longer saw themselves as Irish nationalists first and Labour second, but due to their economic and social circumstances they were rapidly absorbed into the natural constituency which propelled Labour to power. It is even arguable that Labour's growth as a political rival whose appeal was heavily based on social and economic issues forced the Tories to develop their own social programme for government. From then on it seemed that all, or at least most, British politics concerned social and economic issues. It has even been suggested that the abandonment of the twenty-six counties of the Irish Free State was a precondition for the establishment of the British welfare state, as it removed the economic poverty and social conservatism of rural Ireland which could have frustrated the entire experiment. British politics may have been increasingly about class, but at least all parties now *agreed* it was about class. British politicians were now less concerned with trying to reconcile different national aspirations inside the same constitutional structure. Only if Ireland and Irish controversies threatened to come back into British politics would this twentieth-century consensus be disturbed.

Neither Baldwin, Lloyd George nor Macdonald ever again dealt with the boundary issue. MacDonald's only further contact with Ireland was when Eamon de Valera, the Irish Free State leader and a former republican ideologue, sought to overturn the Treaty in the 1930s. De Valera's decision to unpick the Treaty through changes in legislation from 1932 to 1936 by abolishing the Irish Senate, the Oath of Allegiance and the position of Governor-General was greeted with equanimity by Britain, and was another indication that the symbols of British imperialism which were so important in the 1920s had somewhat declined in significance ten years later as Empire metamorphosed into Commonwealth. Whereas in 1922 Winston Churchill was threatening to reinvade the Free State if the anti-Treaty IRA was not dealt with by the Free State government, no such threats were made fifteen years later when de Valera, in effect, tore up many of the underlying principles of the Anglo-Irish Treaty.

Legally, it was no longer possible for Britain to intervene: according to the 1931 Statute of Westminster, Dominions could enact or change legislation without reference to the British parliament. De Valera's constitutional change was accompanied by the Economic War. Britain imposed a twenty-per-cent duty on Free State agricultural products, in retaliation for de Valera refusing to repay land annuities from financial loans that had been granted to Irish tenant farmers by various Land Acts passed by successive British governments. The eventual 1938 settlement, which involved a one-off payment by Ireland to the British of ten million pounds, also involved the transference back to Irish sovereignty of the "Treaty Ports". These had been retained by the British under the Anglo-Irish Treaty in order to protect Britain's western sea approaches. Neither this dispute nor the IRA campaign in Britain in 1939–40 in any way prompted discussion or debate on the Irish border. Nor did, ironically, the formation in 1945 of the Irish Anti-Partition

League (supported by the British Labour Party's Friends of Ireland campaign). Despite its name, the League failed to develop a policy on how the Irish border could be removed. Indeed, it was the British Labour government that, in response to the declaration of the Republic of Ireland Act in Dublin in 1948, passed the Ireland Act of 1949, guaranteeing Northern Ireland's status as part of the UK unless and until the Northern Ireland parliament deemed otherwise. Compared to the magnitude of earlier Irish political turbulence, all of these were merely irritants to the British body politic, extraneous to it – not integral. Above all, nothing was to be said or done that could result in the Irish border and all the historical baggage that went with it returning to the heart of British political life. Discussion of the Irish border had to be avoided at all costs.

In 1939 de Valera declared Irish neutrality in the Second World War in order to avoid invasion (by either the UK or Germany), to stress Irish sovereignty and to avoid reinvigorating old civil war and anti-British sentiments. The declaration of Irish neutrality, as controversial as it was, did not preclude Irish acquiescence in British military use of the waters and airspace of the contested Lough Foyle estuary – which lies between Ireland and Northern Ireland, and remains a disputed territory to this day – and overflying of the Donegal Corridor by British seaplanes travelling west from Fermanagh in Northern Ireland to patrol the North Atlantic. An offer from Britain to end partition if Ireland entered the war on the allied side was treated cautiously when it was revealed that the proposal would have to involve the support of the government of Northern Ireland, which was highly unlikely to be forthcoming.

Neither the IRA's ineffective Border Campaign of the 1950s nor the far more murderous Troubles that were sustained over a thirty-year period in the late twentieth century involved any realistic reconsideration of the Irish border, despite both campaigns having the express ambition to remove the border permanently.

Repartition, and thus a redrawing of the border, did resurface as a potential option at the beginning of the Troubles. The Heath government in the early 1970s and Margaret Thatcher's government in the 1980s both considered (Heath while contemplating a doomsday scenario in the event of communal civil war) the feasibility of transferring nationalist areas and their populations to the Republic of Ireland. In both cases the idea was quickly dismissed as being impractical. It would have to involve widespread transfers of population and a smaller but more Protestant Northern Ireland which would, from a nationalist perspective, ironically have the opposite effect of what was desired: it would reinforce, not weaken, partition. In the 1990s, the idea arose again in a proposal by the Ulster Defence Association that, in the event of British withdrawal from Northern Ireland, Catholic and nationalist areas of Northern Ireland were to be transferred to the Republic, with any nationalists remaining on the "wrong" side of the redrawn border being expelled – or worse. Coming at the height of the Yugoslav Civil War with all its connotations of ethnic cleansing, this proposal was universally condemned.

It is easy to see why such suggestions have been rejected by successive British (and Irish) governments. Not only would they have been highly controversial, but they would also have raised the spectre of the complexity of Irish politics being reintroduced into British mainstream politics once again. Marginal transfers of population, while perhaps desirable in themselves, would have made no substantial impact on the underlying problem. In any event, no such transfers could have taken place under international law without the consent of those involved. More substantial transfers and exchanges of population would have been extremely difficult to achieve and might have resulted only in the creation of two sets of embittered refugees.

Britain's policy of assiduous non-involvement in Ireland unless absolutely necessary would have continued indefinitely if the British referendum on membership of the EU had gone the other way in June 2016. Just as the Anglo-Irish Treaty in 1921 was tacitly accepted in time by all British politicians (even those who vehemently opposed it at first) and was recognised as the key to removing Ireland from the centre of British politics, so the Good Friday Agreement of 1998 quickly assumed the same status as Holy Writ. Even though the Good Friday

Agreement says little about the border and even less about the EU, the expectation was that, as a result of this political agreement, there would be no impediment to movement across the border between the two parts of Ireland. The Agreement's provision for a border poll was to be the equivalent of the Boundary Commission clause in the original Anglo-Irish Treaty; through this device, a decision about whether Ireland would be united would be made at some stage in the future. There would be no need for British political parties to have policies on Irish constitutional issues, as the terms of the Good Friday Agreement would, in time, determine all of this. Consequently, no British political parties have had any meaningful, proactive policies on Ireland. In the same way that the Anglo-Irish Treaty in 1921 seemed to offer British politicians a way out of the Irish morass, so the Good Friday Agreement, underpinned as it was by the EU – which enshrined the principle of no constitutional change in Ireland until the popular will demanded it – provided a similar escape from a similar impasse.

Criticism has been heaped upon, in particular, the English nationalists of the Conservative Party and UKIP for failing to take into account the likely impact of an EU withdrawal decision on a post-Good Friday Agreement Irish border. However, the truth is that no political party in Britain or Ireland expected the outcome of Britain's referendum. Furthermore, this lack of awareness of the possible impact on the

Irish border is hardly surprising, given that it fits exactly with the evolution of British attitudes to Ireland across all political parties over the past century. This "out of sight is out of mind" mindset is exactly the same as the one that allowed the Northern Ireland conflict to creep up again unannounced on British politicians in 1968, when the Troubles began. Equally, it was unrealistic to expect the Leave campaign, driven by such introspective Anglocentric sentiment, to attach much significance to possible knock-on effects on the Celtic fringes of the UK. Anglocentrism is after all a philosophy that, by its nature, pays little attention to internal politics elsewhere. How many English people even have any awareness of what is happening politically in Scotland, a country that shares their island and their state? Under these circumstances, what chance did the Irish border have?

The future of the Irish border is now regarded as being indissolubly linked with the future relationship between the UK and the EU. Because Northern Ireland voted to stay inside the EU in the 2016 referendum, some nationalist politicians have sought to invoke the border poll component of the Good Friday Agreement in order to abolish the Irish border. But the Irish border existed well before the recent referendum, and there is every indication that it will survive long after the Brexit controversy is resolved. Those calling for a border poll now are doing so with the expectation that significant numbers of the unionist middle class, appalled at the prospect of leaving the

EU, will vote to amalgamate with the south in order to preserve their EU citizenship and thus overcome their unionism. This is hardly a realistic assumption, given the lessons and experience of the past hundred years. It assumes that substantial numbers of unionists regard membership of the EU as more important than continued membership of the UK. In fact, the UK subvents Northern Ireland economically to the tune of twelve billion pounds per year, and east–west trade between Northern Ireland and Britain outweighs north–south trade within Ireland by four to one. Recent economic predictions indicate that, in the event of reunification, the quickest and, arguably, only way to make up the subvention shortfall – as the Irish taxpayer is unlikely to manage it – is the immediate removal of forty thousand public service jobs from the Northern Irish economy.

The likelihood is that the future of the Irish border will be determined not by Europe but by the operation of the same atavistic impulses in Northern Ireland which led to its establishment in the first place. In an ideal world, the relationship between the two countries would be the same as that existing between other former dominant powers and their more recalcitrant partners, such as Sweden and Norway (one of which, incidentally, is inside and one outside the EU) or Austria and Italy. As much as both Britain and Ireland would prefer to see the total normalisation of relations between their two states, the future of the Irish border cannot be determined by either of their governments. The Good Friday Agreement is inflexible on the point that the future of the border can only be determined by the decision of the people who live in Northern Ireland. It therefore follows that a state, even if it wanted to, could not legally expel up to a million of its citizens against their will.

It follows that if Irish nationalists wish to remove the Irish border, they will have to persuade Ulster unionists to agree to do so. In the not-too-distant past, Irish republicans expected British politicians, particularly in the British Labour Party, to do their convincing for them by becoming proxy persuaders for Irish unity. If one accepts that unionists are unlikely to be convinced by a supposedly reformed version of the same kind of militant republicanism that they have recently experienced, it therefore falls to mainstream Irish nationalists to do the work of persuasion instead. However, the basic problem is that the history of Irish nationalism is one of antagonism towards the idea of unionism being a valid political philosophy in Ireland. Irish nationalism was born in the late nineteenth century as part of the rise in nationalism throughout Europe at that time. The idea that "the people" was a single unit defined by its cultural and linguistic distinctiveness and entitled to its God-given "natural" territory is only now being challenged in post-nationalist Ireland. This concept of nationalism also defined itself by what it was not – in Ireland's case, British. Other national entities in Europe resolved the problem of recalcitrant minorities, particularly in the mayhem of continental Europe after the First World War, by expulsion and forced transfer of populations. This did not happen on anything like the European scale in Ireland (although there was substantial Protestant flight to both Northern Ireland and Britain after 1922). In Ireland, the principles of ethnic nationalism were theoretically underpinned by an older philosophy of secular republicanism uniting Irish people irrespective of religious affiliation.

The new Irish state, however, was largely based on nineteenth-century principles of national identity – exclusivist, Catholic, Gaelic and rural, rather than the democratic, inclusive, secular republicanism of the US and France. It was perhaps inevitable after such a lengthy period under British domination that the new state was to base its identity on what it meant to be Irish, on those characteristics which were the total opposite of being British. However, the effect was to further alienate the one-fifth of the population who defined themselves as that opposite which was so anathema to Irish nationalism. If Irish unionists rejected more moderate and pragmatic nationalists such as the Home Rulers they were hardly likely to be attracted to the more purist and ideological nationalists who often identified their nationalism, partially at least, in terms of not being British.

For most of the twentieth century, Irish nationalists hardly made any attempt to reconcile their version of Ireland with the unionists' version. The old nostrums did start to break down after 1973, when the south began to embrace the social and economic secularism that came with joining the European Economic Community. However, there has been little real effort on the part of nationalist Ireland to break out of its former cosy homogeneity and relative political tranquillity in a sustained attempt to attract northern unionists. This is perhaps surprising given that the ethnic, religious and linguistic conformity and homogeneity that characterised the southern state for most of its existence has itself now been transformed into a vibrant modern multiculturalism. That multiculturalism, though, seems not to include the Britishness which has been such a feature of Irishness for so long. Embracing such Britishness seems to be a step too far for Irish nationalists. This is unfortunate given the historical, linguistic, social, cultural and economic links that have bound the two countries together over the lengthy history of their relationship. There seems to be little enthusiasm for the need to, for example, craft a brand new Irish constitution if and when the border disappears. At the very least this constitution would have to give formal recognition to symbols of Britishness, such as the Commonwealth and the Monarchy which are so important to the Protestant psyche. Then again, would the effort of devising a new constitution be worth it? It would undoubtedly create substantial controversy, with the prospect of very little return if northern unionists were to reject it. In asking unionists to give up the union, are

Irish nationalists prepared to sacrifice total separation for the unity of Ireland? Which is more important: a completely independent republic or Irish unity? This is the same question that dominated the Anglo-Irish Treaty debates in Dublin nearly a century ago, and it is still as controversial and uncomfortable now as it was then. It is depressing that, after nearly a century of independence, Irish nationalism still lacks sufficient self-confidence to interpret emblems of Britishness – membership of the Commonwealth, for example – as anything other than a threat. India, which became independent a quarter of a century after Ireland and whose founding fathers derived so much inspiration from Ireland's example, does not see membership of the Commonwealth as endangering its republican principles. Nor is it motivated by a negative Anglophobia in the way that much of nationalist Ireland still is. The conclusion can only be that Irish nationalists' outreach to their separated brethren in the north is still very much a work in progress.

Equally, Ulster unionists will have to reach out to their nationalist fellow citizens in the north if they want to ensure that the border survives much beyond its centenary. The border was established to ensure a permanent Protestant and unionist majority in the new state. British politics may have moved on and the old Civil War politics may have disappeared, even in the south, but the central political issue in Northern Ireland remains the same as it was nearly a hundred years ago. At that time, there was no incentive, let alone the slightest inclination, to attract reluctant Catholics to the new state. The demographic picture has now dramatically changed due to the increased Catholic birth rate and the flight to Britain of the university-educated Protestant middle class. With delicious piquancy, the number of Catholics in Northern Ireland is predicted to equal the number of Protestants in 2021, the same year that the border reaches its hundredth anniversary. However, it has been conjectured that if Catholics become numerically dominant it might be an attractive proposition for them to vote to remain in the union, where they would now be in the majority while at the same time being able to continue to avail of superior public services compared to the south. Therefore, predictions that the future of the border will depend on a straightforward sectarian headcount may be wide of the mark.

From a unionist perspective, in order for the border to remain there has to be a move from an ethnic to a civic unionism, and an active appeal to Catholics to support the union. Depressingly, unionists so far seem to have been largely reticent in reaching out to argue their case to non-unionists, but there have been recent indications that some progressive unionists are prepared to argue for agreed cross-community processes and timetables to be established for the future governance of Northern Ireland (and indeed Ireland) rather than continually fixating on the immediate controversies that separate the communities and perpetuate political crisis.

Will the Irish border survive? In 1912 the proposal that

within a decade a border would be dividing Ireland into two states would have been (and was) treated with incredulity. Even the most ardent unionist supporters of partition in 1921 could not have contemplated that that border would still be in existence nearly a century later. It was expected that it was a temporary arrangement in order to overcome an immediate political crisis. Unionists could (and did) always point out that Ireland has only ever been united under British rule, and that the political reunification of Ireland could be achieved as part of a new constitutional arrangement between Ireland and Britain. However, after a hundred years of Irish independence, the prospects of the Republic of Ireland joining a federation of Britain and Ireland, as has been suggested by some unionist and British Conservative commentators, seems somewhat remote, especially given recent political developments in Britain – even if federation could facilitate the reunification of Ireland and abolish the border. The irony is that the peaceful breaking down of borders was once argued as a reason for both Ireland and Britain joining Europe in the first place.

The credit or blame (depending on perspective) for the existence of the Irish border must be shared by all British political parties as well as by the competing nationalisms in Ireland. A border which was originally a county border is now an international border, and although originally intended to be temporary it is still there nearly a hundred years later. This border can only be removed by the democratic will of the electorate in both parts of Ireland, and that will can be expressed no more than once every seven years. In 1987 I witnessed Berlin preparing to celebrate forty years as the capital of East Germany. The communist state looked impregnable. It showed no sign of collapse. Two years later the Berlin Wall came down, and three years later the German Democratic Republic was no more. The speed of this collapse was indeed breathtaking. There is no evidence that the same will happen to the Irish border. But in a united Germany twenty-five years later, the mental and psychological border between east and west remains. The Irish border has been in existence for nearly a century – over twice the length of time the German border existed. In addition, it was not imposed peremptorily from outside, against the wishes of a unified nation, as the German border was. The appearance of the Irish border in 1921 reflected centuries of cultural, ethnic and religious difference between the two parts of Ireland. It would be unrealistic to expect that if the Irish border were removed the same psychological separateness would not continue to be experienced between the two parts of Ireland for decades to come. The psychological impact of the border should not be underestimated. It symbolised certainty and security for the unionist majority inside it. However, because of this majority's inability and unwillingness to welcome their nationalist neighbours as equal citizens, the same border became a symbol of discrimination and a constant reminder to nationalists of their second-class status.

Paradoxically, it was through benefitting from the advanced social and educational standards of the British welfare state as extended to Northern Ireland that the nationalist population came to no longer be prepared to tolerate their second-class status. This was evidenced by the growth of a substantial Catholic middle class expecting to be treated as equal citizens in Northern Ireland, and first manifested dramatically in the late 1960s with the birth of the civil rights movement. The concept of equality that emerged then (colloquially known as "parity of esteem") became, thirty years later, the cornerstone of the Good Friday Agreement.

For the first fifty years of Northern Ireland's existence, it was in the political and economic interest of the unionist majority to maintain a secure border. This security aspect intensified during the Troubles of the late twentieth century even as, paradoxically, the economic necessity of the border dissolved with the arrival of the European Single Market. Following the Good Friday Agreement in 1998, for the past twenty years, there has been no visible Irish border. The political, social and economic impact of this is significant – all parties involved in the current Brexit debate in Ireland, Britain and the EU have indicated that they do not wish to see restrictions of movement across the border reimposed. However, there remains a real possibility that at least some economic barriers will once again be reinstated.

Prior to the result of the Brexit referendum there was

evidence that, because of greater equality, increased prosperity and more sophisticated public services in Northern Ireland following the Good Friday Agreement, more Catholics in Northern Ireland were becoming reconciled to their position inside the UK. However, uncertainty on this issue may have increased as a result of the Brexit vote; the loss of EU citizenship, allied to traditional affinity with the south, may persuade more nationalists in Northern Ireland to vote for Irish unity than otherwise would have been the case. This will only become apparent if a poll on the future of the Irish border takes place – but it cannot be overemphasised that the future of the Irish border can only be determined by the electorates of both parts of Ireland agreeing its future.

Ironically, in its attempts to leave the EU Britain is, for the first time in a century, forced to re-engage with the politics of the Irish border. It remains to be seen how this will play out, but this time it will no longer be possible for Britain to distance itself from any involvement as it has for nearly a century. To paraphrase Thomas Jones, Ireland is now well and truly back in British politics.

Acknowledgements

I have been fascinated by the Irish border since studying political and historical geography at Queen's University Belfast many years ago. Thanks to Dr Neville Douglas and Dr Robin Glasscock for developing this interest in the Irish border. Thanks also to Professor Michael Laffan, Dr Kevin Matthews and Professor Ged Martin for permitting me to use and quote from their excellent accounts on the history of the Irish border. Thanks also to my wife Hilda McCafferty and former BBC Political Correspondent Nicholas Jones for persuading me to write this book explaining, in the words of Thomas Jones, the Deputy Cabinet Secretary to four British Prime Ministers, why "Ireland is now back in our politics".

Notes

1   Quoted in Michael Laffan, *The Partition of Ireland 1911–1925* (Dundalgan Press, 1983), p 13

2   Quoted in Alan O'Day, *Irish Home Rule 1867–1921* (Manchester University Press, 1998), p 182

3   Quoted in Laffan, *The Partition*, p 16

4   Quoted in Laffan, *The Partition*, p 46

5   Quoted in Laffan, *The Partition*, p 60

6   Quoted in Kevin Matthews, *Fatal Influence: The Impact of Ireland on British Politics, 1920–1925* (University College Dublin Press, 2004), p 2

7   *Articles of agreement for a Treaty between Great Britain and Ireland* (His Majesty's Stationery Office, 1921), article 12

8   A J P Taylor, *English History: 1914–1945* (Clarendon Press, 1965), p 236

9   Quoted in Ged Martin, "The Origins of Partition", in Malcolm Anderson and Eberhard Bort eds, *The Irish Border: History, Politics, Culture* (Liverpool University Press, 1999), p 57

10 Thomas Jones, *Whitehall Diary: Volume 3, Ireland 1918–25*, Keith Middlemas ed (Oxford University Press, 1971), p 234

11 Quoted in Richard Toye, *Winston Churchill: Politics, Strategy and Statecraft* (Bloomsbury Academic, 2017), p 58
12 Parliament of Northern Ireland, HC Deb 24 April 1935, vol 16, col 1095

HAUS CURIOSITIES

Inspired by the topical pamphlets of the interwar years, as
well as by Einstein's advice to 'never lose a holy curiosity',
the series presents short works of opinion and analysis by
notable figures. Under the guidance of the series editor, Peter
Hennessy, Haus Curiosities have been published since 2014.

Welcoming contributions from a diverse pool of authors, the series
aims to reinstate the concise and incisive booklet as a powerful
strand of politico-literary life, amplifying the voices of those
who have something urgent to say about a topical theme.

'Nifty little essays – the thinking person's commuting read'
– *The Independent*

ALSO IN THIS SERIES

Britain in a Perilous World:
The Strategic Defence and Security Review We Need
by Jonathan Shaw

The UK's In-Out Referendum: EU Foreign and Defence Policy Reform
by David Owen

Establishment and Meritocracy
by Peter Hennessy

Greed: From Gordon Gekko to David Hume
by Stewart Sutherland

*The Kingdom to Come: Thoughts on the Union
Before and After the Scottish Referendum*
by Peter Hennessy

Commons and Lords: A Short Anthropology of Parliament
by Emma Crewe

*The European Identity:
Historical and Cultural Realities We Cannot Deny*
by Stephen Green

Breaking Point: The UK Referendum on the EU and its Aftermath
by Gary Gibbon

Brexit and the British: Who Are We Now?
by Stephen Green

These Islands: A Letter to Britain
by Ali M. Ansari

Lion and Lamb: A Portrait of British Moral Duality
By Mihir Bose

*The Power of Civil Servants
(published with Westminster Abbey Institute)*
by David Normington and Peter Hennessy

The Power of Politicians (published with Westminster Abbey Institute)
by Tessa Jowell and Frances D'Souza

The Power of Journalists (published with Westminster Abbey Institute)
by Nick Robinson, Barbara Speed, Charlie Beckett and Gary Gibbon

The Power of Judges (published with Westminster Abbey Institute)
by David Neuberger and Peter Riddell